S0-BLP-524

i can DECORATE
furniture
rejuvenation

# Economical
## and ecological

Breathing new life into old furniture is not an arduous task. It requires a modest budget and talent, even limited. It really comes down to mastering the correct techniques and properly handling the materials. This guide will lead you by the hand without hindering your creativity. Let's challenge the "throw-away trend" by *recycling*.

*Poetic phrases have inspired masterpieces like this armoire, which can easily be found in most large department stores.*

RESEARCH AND STYLING: NATHALIE JOLICŒUR. PHOTOGRAPHY: MARTIN HOUDE, PRATICO MEDIA.

The word "recycling" is an integral part of our everyday speech. The process goes beyond placing tin cans and stacks of papers in a recycling bin. In fact, recycling also includes rummaging around second-hand stores and flea markets to find furniture that can be salvaged, restored and then used to embellish your own décor.

Searching through your attic or basement might lead to the discovery of long-forgotten castaways. Or, how about reinventing a shelving unit that has forever been part of your home's décor? In short, recycling allows you to look at furniture from a different perspective, with a view to transforming it and thus increase its life expectancy.

Techniques to accomplish this task continue to multiply. Stripping allows the wood's original charm to shine through or prepares the surface for a new finish. Paints and stains confer a new, rejuvenated appearance.

Also, interesting fabrics or picture collages can infuse new life into furniture that has seen better days. Another option is to integrate ceramic tiles or other materials. Wood trim and accessories also have the knack of reviving dressers or armoires that, over time, have lost their appeal.

Not only that, it's possible to completely redefine the nature and utilization of furniture through refurbishing. This transformation can involve removing sections, adding sections or even combining two pieces of furniture to fashion a new one.

*The original marble tabletop was replaced with a more inviting finish that is better suited to the kitchen's style. Only the wrought-iron table base was retained. The appetizing fruit arrangement depicted on the tabletop's wooden surface is the creation of a talented artist. The new cushions and theme-appropriate motifs on the chairs complement the décor perfectly.*

RESEARCH: NATHALIE JOLICŒUR. STYLING: GUYLAINE ST-AMAND. PHOTOGRAPHY: MARTIN HOUDE, PRATICO MEDIA.

*This design is ideal for anyone blessed with a talent for painting. The fruit seems so ripe and appetizing; one is almost tempted to take a bite!*

In short, this guide is meant to be an idea kit as well as a toolbox where you can browse for inspiration. To help you successfully complete your projects, these makeovers are explained and illustrated in step-by-step detail, from the surface preparation to the final finish.

But, first and foremost, this guide abounds with sound advice and ingenious tricks of the trade. Each transformation process is explained in detail to ensure a professional result. Whether you are working with wood or melamine, the various techniques will be appropriate and job-specific.

As you can see, furniture rejuvenation is an art form that is accessible to everyone because we all possess the raw material needed to succeed: imagination. Since this endeavour is as enjoyable as it is gratifying, it makes for a great pastime. However, to fully appreciate it, you must know what you are doing.

# JAPANESE RESTYLING

**S**imple and aesthetically Zen, the front of this storage unit is in perfect harmony with the rest of the design! The trimwork and bamboo inserts displayed on each compartment convey a unique charm. This piece of furniture elegantly occupies the space beneath the flat-screen television. The two elements unite to become the room's focal point.

*Believe or not, this piece of furniture, minus the top half, was the starting point for this design.*

*What a clever use of mouldings! Here, a frame was affixed to the unit's top outside edges to create a recessed area in the centre. This space, between the glass and the furniture's surface, houses two decorative bamboo panels and an assortment of stones.*

RESEARCH: NATHALIE JOLICŒUR. STYLING: GUYLAINE ST-AMAND. PHOTOGRAPHY: MARTIN HOUDE, PRATICO MEDIA.

*The different components of the design are illustrated here. Mouldings create a frame on which a bevelled glass top rests, protecting the decorative display inside the recessed area. Photographs or an extra-large scrapbooking project could be interesting alternatives.*

# MODIGLIANI APPROACH

**T**hrough the magic of an artist's paintbrush, this kitchen table has become a work of art. This masterpiece melds so well with this creatively inspired universe that one might overlook its utilitarian attributes. Superb and exceptional are the right words to describe the achieved result.

RESEARCH: NATHALIE JOLICŒUR. STYLING: GUYLAINE ST-AMAND. PHOTOGRAPHY: MARTIN HOUDE, PRATICO MEDIA.

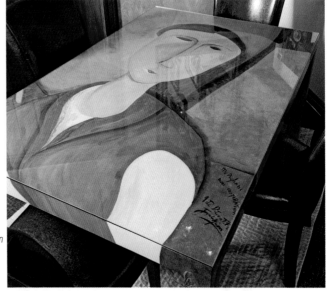

*This Modigliani-inspired representation of a woman was painted on an ordinary melamine surface. The breathtaking beauty of this unique work of art is unrivalled.*

# Restoring wood

Each coat of paint has a TALL TALE to tell! Hospital green coincides with the birth of our youngest, while the baby pink era corresponds to Lucy's room. Flaming orange made its appearance at the same time as dad's moustache. While restoring wood, you'll get the chance to reminisce over some fond memories. From STRIPPING to the final finish, discover USEFUL PRODUCTS that will help breathe new life into your old furniture.

**BEFORE**

*This dresser is accented with interesting detailing, which was almost impossible to notice under the many layers of paint.*

*No, it's not your imagination! This elegant dresser, which looks like it belongs in an antique shop, was simply restored. Now, it blends in beautifully with the room's countrified environment.*

RESEARCH: NATHALIE JOLICŒUR. STYLING: GUYLAINE ST-AMAND. PHOTOGRAPHY: MARTIN HOUDE, PRATICO MEDIA.

# TYPES OF STRIPPING PRODUCTS

Paint and varnish stripping products (also referred to as paint & varnish removers) are numerous and their ideal utilization differs. The following text describes them briefly. These products can be used for interior and exterior use. Among the examples presented, only one is described as a biodegradable product.

## Spray-on

This type of furniture stripper is ideal for used furniture covered with paint or varnish. It is also perfectly adaptable to stained furniture because it is applied as a spray. As such, the particles penetrate the wood grain easily, which in turn loosen the stain with greater ease. Furthermore, it is most convenient for the less accessible areas of a piece of furniture. This remover does not leak and can eliminate two to three coats at a time.

### READ THE LABELS

**Never use a stripping product without reading the manufacturer's instructions. The labels provide you with specific information on surface preparation, required application tools, dissolving and cleaning processes, as well as the appropriate drying time.**

## The "Intelligent" stripping product

Here is a fantastic product when you are unaware of the history behind the piece of furniture. How many coats of paint are there? Has it been varnished or stained? With this particular product, it actually doesn't matter because this type of furniture stripper recognizes the types of finishes that are present and makes them disappear, three to five coats at a time.

## Super Décapant

This product is strong and acts swiftly. It can remove four to five coats without risking damaging the wood.

## Furniture stripper

Other fast-acting, multi-coat liquid strippers also exist. They are used for a multitude of tasks, but their use is often reserved for flat surfaces with small crevices.

## Mild stripper

Ecological and biodegradable, there are no fumes to worry about with this product. It does, however, require more than one application to do the job because it is less powerful than others. In addition, it remains wet in comparison to other strippers that tend to dry when left too long on the surface. Its odour is also milder than other products.

## Paste-type

The paste furniture stripper has a thicker texture than other furniture strippers, because it contains a larger quantity of paraffin. It works miracles on vertical surfaces. Nonetheless, it has to soak for a longer period of time due to its consistency.

### PROTECT YOURSELF!

**You must take care to protect yourself properly before you tackle a furniture stripping job. Considering their potency, stripping products are harmful to your skin and health. It is therefore important to wear neoprene gloves as well as safety glasses. You must also protect the floor with a tarp or drop sheet. Lastly, it is necessary to work in a well-ventilated area, or better yet, wait until you can work outdoors.**

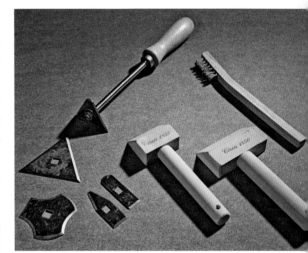

### Stripping tools

*A wide selection of scrapers is available on the market. Among them, the wooden types are highly recommended. Their rounded edges prevent damage to your furniture's surface. A scraper with an interchangeable head is helpful for dealing with curves, motifs or areas that are difficult to reach. The brass-bristle brush helps loosen the paint in the wood fibres without scratching the surface. The stripping heat gun, which does not appear on the picture, is equipped with an element that heats the paint and raises it from the surface. You must handle this tool with care because it can brown or blacken the wood if the heat applied is too intense. All being said and done, the use of a scraper remains necessary to complete the task.*

## Neutralizers

Considering that stripping products contain active ingredients, it is important to neutralize those agents. To do so, soak a piece of steel wool in a lacquer thinner, methyl hydrate (wood alcohol), mineral spirit or water, as per the manufacturer's instructions on the product label. Scrub the surface in the same direction as the wood grain. This will loosen the residue left by the stripping product, contaminants or greasy deposits. In fact, this step neutralizes the stripping product's active ingredients, preventing the stain and varnish from staying wet, and ensures that a cloudy film does not appear later. Finally, let the piece of furniture dry for 24 hours to ensure that all active agents have been neutralized. Note that some stripping products do not require any neutralizer.

# REMOVING THE OLD FINISH

Suffocating under all these coats of paint, the wood can no longer breathe. Stripping allows the wood to free itself from this unwanted shell. Starting with its natural and smooth surface, a new finish can be applied. Of course, eliminating all traces of paint might seem difficult. Keep in mind though that the task will be easier if you use the proper tools such as those shown in the following step-by-step instructions.

## MY ADVICE

**B**efore stripping, the task at hand must be assessed. To do this, start by stripping a small section in a less visible area so that you can closely examine the wood. This process will provide you with clues on the former finish, the type of wood and its condition. Then, you can make a decision as to whether you should strip the piece of furniture or simply clean it and touch it up. Of course, it is important to consider the age of each piece of furniture. An antique piece of great value should not be used as your first experiment. You also need to remove the hardware and accessories. If they cannot be removed, protect them with masking tape. Lastly, consider the extent of repairs needed, if applicable.

*Apply the first coat of remover with an old paintbrush. Let the stripping product penetrate according to the length of time recommended by the manufacturer. Next, use a wooden scraper to eliminate any residue. To avoid damaging the wood, take care to scrape the surface in the same direction as the wood grain. This step can be repeated if any residue remains on the surface.*

*2 Use a brass-bristle brush to remove the paint on motif-decorated or textured surfaces.*

*3 Use a scraper with an interchangeable head to strip the areas that are more difficult to access.*

*4 Pour on another coat of remover. Scrub the surface with steel wool to eliminate all traces of stain, varnish or paint. As always, rub in the same direction as the wood grain. Neutralize the surface with a cloth soaked in whichever neutralizer is recommended by the manufacturer. Allow it to dry as per the recommended time.*

## SANDING

A surface that is well-prepared absorbs the finishing product uniformly. That is why sanding is an essential part of the task. For effective results, it is important to select the correct sandpaper grit. Coarser grits, from #60 to #100, eliminate the old finish. Medium-grit sandpaper, from #120 to #150, is used for the preliminary sanding stage, and #180 to #220-grit sandpaper is used for the final sanding step. Fine-grit sandpaper, from #300 to #400, is designed for sanding between coats of varnish, and #600 is for the final finishing coat.

*This step can be performed with an electric sander, which must be used with care. In fact, this tool can dig into the surface if you are moving against the grain or if you hold it on the same spot for too long. Otherwise, sanding can very well be completed by hand.*

*For the first sanding step, use 100-grit sandpaper. Next, fill the holes with wood filler. If you are going to stain a piece of furniture, make sure that the wood filler used can be stained. If you plan on varnishing a piece of furniture without staining first, use wood filler of a similar colour to the wood. Allow it to dry and continue. The following sanding step requires 120-grit sandpaper and the last stage requires 150-grit. As you move through the sanding steps, you are advised not to skip more than one grit-size from one step to the other, and to always sand in the same direction as the wood grain. This will prevent imperfections and the finish will be much more successful. To facilitate the task, use sanding blocks for rounded surfaces. Once sanding is complete, use a resin cloth to clean the surface and remove the dust.*

## PRESTAINING: A MUST

For quality work, it is recommended to use a prestain product before actually staining the wood. This product helps maintain uniformity with respect to stain penetration in the fibre. The application must always be performed in the same direction as the wood grain, on a clean, dry and dust-free surface. If using a water-based product, it is necessary to sand the surface lightly with fine-grit sandpaper before graduating to the staining process. A few minutes after applying the product to the piece of furniture, wipe off all excess with a cloth. Wait at least 30 minutes before staining the surface. Note that oil-based prestain products usually require an oil-based stain. The same logic applies to water-based products.

*This picture clearly reveals the potential colour variation when the prestaining step is omitted. This marble effect results from the fact that the wood has absorbed the stain in various degrees.*

*Prestaining allows the stain to penetrate uniformly into the wood.*

# CHOOSING A NEW FINISH

Stain enhances the appearance of the wood – it colours it without masking the grain. Since it is simply a matter of aesthetics, its use is a matter of choice. If you are satisfied with the natural shade of the wood, feel free to skip the staining step and proceed directly to varnishing.

Unlike paint, stain penetrates the wood. Therefore, the colour must be chosen with care as it is difficult to reverse the process once it's applied. When selecting the hue, you must take the type of wood into consideration. There are different levels of wood fibre porosity and each will absorb staining products in their own way.

## my solution

Before applying stain to an entire piece of furniture, it is best to perform a test in a non-visible area to determine your colour preference. This test must be performed after the application of the prestain product. Following this simple precaution prevents disappointments and results in savings on the purchase of stain.

*Not all wood types absorb products the same way. Furthermore, each variety boasts its own natural colour. Here, the same stain colour was applied to different types of wood. From left to right, you have pine, maple, birch and oak.*

*A good finish must both embellish and preserve the wood. This is achieved by applying several layers of various products, understanding that each product has its own purpose. A typical finish consists of three coats: prestain (1), stain (2) and varnish (3). Can you see how the varnish enhances the appearance of the stain?*

*The final stain colour can vary according to the type of wood. Here you can see the difference between six colours from the Saman brand name, (from left to right: olive, sesame, walnut, amaretto, spice and chocolate) which were applied respectively to pine, walnut, birch and oak (from top to bottom).*

# STAIN TYPES

Basically, there are two categories of stains: water-based and oil-based. The products available on the market come in varying textures (liquid, gel or paste) and each one boasts its own interesting characteristics. Learn more in the following text.

### Oil-based stain

*An oil-based stain emits a strong, unpleasant odour, but it is easy to apply and deeply penetrates wood. Its pigments offer a more uniform and natural colour. The application is performed with a cloth until the desired tint is achieved. Drying time can take up to 24 hours. This product does not require wiping after the application.*

### Water-based stain

*Water, latex or acrylic-based products have the same characteristics. These types of products are more difficult to apply than oil-based stains, but they do not emit any odour. They are applied with a sponge or a polyester-bristle paintbrush and the excess is wiped off with a cloth. Since this stain dries very quickly, it must be applied swiftly and to small sections at a time.*

### Gel stain

*Gel stain is usually oil-based. Because of its unique texture, it does not run, which makes it ideal for vertical surfaces. It is applied copiously with a clean cloth and the excess is wiped off with a cotton cloth. In comparison to liquid products, gel stain does require additional surface wiping.*

### Stain/varnish

*This two-in-one product, usually oil-based, combines colour and protection in a single step. Once thoroughly mixed, you apply a very thin coat with a paintbrush, taking care to do so as evenly as possible, and there is no need to wipe off after the application. Once the drying time has elapsed, it requires light sanding with 400-grit sandpaper. This operation can be repeated if you wish to obtain a more vivid colour.*

# STAINING TOOLS

*Various tools are needed to apply stain: a paintbrush with 100% natural-silk bristles (1) for oil-based products; a polyester-bristle paintbrush (2) for water, latex or acrylic-based stains; an artist paintbrush (3) for touch-ups and for hard-to-reach areas, and a lint-free staining cloth (4), which is effective with all products. Cotton mesh (5), cheesecloth (6) and sponges (7) all perform well. This is where your personal preference comes into play.*

### MY ADVICE

**C**hildren, pregnant women and people affected with respiratory disorders must avoid being exposed to products emitting volatile organic compounds (VOCs). It is best to refrain from using products that contain such compounds.

*Before and during use, shake the product vigorously to prevent the colorant from sticking to the bottom of the container. Wear latex gloves. With a stain cloth or another type of cloth, apply the product following the direction of the wood grain. If using water-based stain, wait approximately 20 seconds and then wipe the surface thoroughly with a clean dry cloth. Should you find that a second coat is necessary in order to accent the stain, take care to respect the drying time recommended by the manufacturer before proceeding.*

# THE FINAL COAT

After so much care has been taken to the finishing process, it is only natural to protect the stain with a varnish. This will protect the surface from scratches and wear and tear. As for the large variety of stains, several types of varnishes and textures are available.

Before using such a finishing product, it is important to ensure that it is compatible with the stain previously applied. Each product is formulated for a particular use and has its own characteristics. The following text contains a description of a few of these products.

*From left to right, the photo shows examples of types of finish: matte, satin, semi-gloss and high gloss. As a general rule, the higher the gloss, the more visible any defect will be. The matte finish becomes glossier with time. The satin and semi-gloss finishes are therefore an excellent trade-off. Shown in the two containers are the oil-based varnish (on the left) and the water-based varnish (on the right). Oil-based varnish is easy to apply and offers a smoother finish, but yellows quickly and its drying time is extremely long. On the other hand, water-based varnish dries quickly, does not yellow over time and emits practically no odour. Special care is required during application to avoid brush-stroke marks. Remember that you must not shake a liquid varnish container. It is best to stir the varnish with a paint stick to lift the deposits from the bottom of the container.*

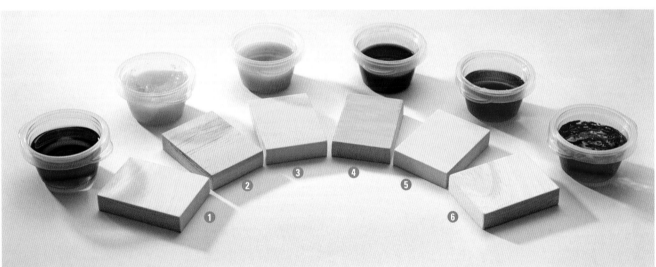

*Other finishing products are also sold on the market. These products can be a good substitute for varnish, but they are not all durable and may be difficult to clean. Their characteristics are:*

**①** *Boiled linseed oil does not alter the natural colour of the wood. In fact, it enhances the appearance of the wood grain. This product is ideal for obtaining an antique finish.*

**②** *Furniture wax is mainly formulated from beeswax, carnauba wax or both. It protects the wood and prevents it from drying out. Its application must be repeated several times a year. The product is sold as a paste, gel, liquid or spray.*

**③** *and* **④** *Shellac provides a classic natural finish. This product can darken over the years. As shown in the picture, shellac can be transparent or can have an amber colour. It is worthwhile to point out that its application is more laborious.*

**⑤** *Tung oil is used as frequently for indoor furniture as it is for outdoor furniture. It is proven to be durable and water-resistant as well as alkalis-resistant. It is easy to apply and does not change colour over time.*

**⑥** *Paste varnish is formulated from a polyurethane-based gel. It provides a smooth lustre and a durable finish. It does not leak when the application is performed on vertical surfaces. This product proves to be very practical when repairing a small section of a piece of furniture. It also offers great resistance to moisture.*

*After staining a piece of furniture, wait 24 to 48 hours before applying varnish. For the first coat, it is recommended not to go over the same area twice in order to avoid diluting the stain. Use 400-grit sandpaper and sand the surface lightly after each coat of varnish. Then, remove the dust particles with a resin cloth. To better protect your wood, two to three coats of varnish is recommended.*

# Transforming melamine

Bored with white melamine, you say! Rest assured, you are not alone.

There's an abundance of melamine furniture around that is still in great

shape. Melamine is a survivor, although not always in style. Almost any

piece of furniture deserves a second chance, even those made

of melamine. With a little imagination and the proper surface preparation,

even your unwanted dresser can exude a new

charm that will seduce you all over again.

*This storage unit showcases an attractive array of shapes. Triangles and rectangles can live in harmony. Is anything better than furniture that offers both functionality and great appeal?*

RESEARCH: NATHALIE JOLICŒUR. STYLING: GUYLAINE ST-AMAND.
PHOTOGRAPHY: MARTIN HOUDE, PRATICO MEDIA.

*What a makeover! This bookcase was the design's starting point, proving that anything can be rejuvenated.*

BEFORE

D<small>o</small> you have any doubts that melamine can be painted in order to achieve a successful transformation? To prove this is possible, this section invites you to give it a try! By following the proposed technique, the preparatory steps and the drying time, the final outcome will surprise you. Even better, the finish will stand the test of time.

*Required material: T.S.P. or TSPe; 120-grit and 400-grit sandpaper, oil-based primer; 5/8" white melamine; white veneer edge strip (trim); 1/4" x 2" pine moulding; Richelieu (brand name) handles #391203193, four interior hinges for melamine and four suspension arms; all-purpose glue; wood filler; nails and screws.*

*Finish: Saman (brand name) wood effect kit, walnut colour (for the furniture piece) and stain colour #119 (for the mouldings); water-based varnish with matte finish.*

*Required tools: clean cloth; latex gloves; old paintbrush; staining cloth; paintbrush with 100% natural-silk bristles; polyester-bristle paintbrush, table saw; pencil; measuring tape; mitre saw; clothing iron; drill; air-powered nail gun or hammer.*

*Step-by-step instructions:*

✔ *To create the new door panels, measure the distance from side to side and between the shelves. Measure and cut the new melamine panels with the table saw. Subtract 1/4" from the measured length and width to ensure that the panels fit properly into the openings. With a clothing iron, apply the veneer trim to the sides. These door panels will close the centre and bottom compartments.*

✔ *In the upper compartment, measure a full diagonal line and cut the shelf with the table saw. Cut the ends at an angle. Insert the shelf and measure the other two diagonal lines. Cut the two last shelves and affix them from the corners to the full-length diagonal shelf with all-purpose glue and finishing nails. Apply the veneer trim to the front only.*

✔ *Prepare the melamine surface (see steps below).*

✔ *Proceed with the finishing steps for the melamine (see steps on following page).*

✔ *Take your measurements for the mouldings and cut them to size. Apply stain #119 with a staining cloth. Please note that the Saman stain formula does not require prestaining. Allow it to dry. Apply two coats of the water-based varnish with a polyester-bristle paintbrush. Affix the mouldings to the doors with all-purpose glue. Secure them with finishing nails. Fill the holes and joints with wood filler. Make the necessary staining touch-ups.*

✔ *Install the hinges, suspension arms and handles.*

## MY ADVICE

T<small>o</small> keep the melamine from chipping while cutting, cut your panels with the interior side facing up. As such, trace your cutting lines on the panels' interior face. Adjust the saw blade 1/8" higher than the panels' thickness. This way, there will be less mechanical effort from the blade and motor because more of the blade's teeth will go through the piece at once. If the blade is too high, it will enter head-first and in full force into the material, which is good to avoid.

## PREPARING THE MELAMINE

1 *First and foremost, you need to clean any grease and dust from the surface. For a thorough cleaning, use T.S.P. (a cleaning product containing trisodium phosphate). As this is a toxic product, you must wear gloves and carefully follow the manufacturer's instructions. Once cleaning is complete, rinse the surface with clear water several times to remove any remaining oily residue. If you use TSPe, dilute the product as per the manufacturer's instructions. Apply this product with a rag, wipe any excess and allow it to dry. Note that this product does not require rinsing. If you change or reposition the handles, fill the holes on both sides of the panels with wood filler.*

2 *With 120-grit sandpaper, remove all imperfections and the melamine's glossy finish. Sand in the same direction as the faux finish you plan on applying. Make sure to remove all dust particles with a clean cloth. If you plan on applying the same finish to the mouldings, install them before tackling the next step.*

3 *Use a foam roller or a paintbrush with 100% natural-silk bristles to apply one coat of oil-based primer. There are also some 100% acrylic primers that adhere well to melamine. Note that you can limit the number of base coats by having your primer tinted the same colour as your paint. It is advised to apply the primer and the base coat uniformly and in the same direction. If not, paint streaks could appear once the work is complete.*

## THE SECRET TO A PERFECT FINISH

The finish is what conveys the impression of a successfully completed project. Here is some useful advice for brilliant results:

- Foam paintbrushes and rollers are first-choice tools to successfully achieve a smooth and more natural finish.
- For a lacquered finish, floor urethane is ideal. This type of finish proves to be durable and glossy (approximately 70% lustre).
- Looking for a faux finish? Take a stroll through the painting product aisles to discover the wide variety of tools fashioned to create numerous effects. Note that a mixture of paint colour and glaze is needed to achieve a faux finish. Apply the primer and the finishing coat with good-quality paintbrushes. When proceeding with a faux finish, keep in mind that maintaining the same directional movements will avoid the appearance of streaks once the work is complete. Finally, it is important to protect your work with a varnish with either a matte or low sheen finish.

*Simple hinges allowed for the addition of door panels to the shelving unit. The enclosed sections make it easier to keep a tidy, clean look.*

## FINISHING STEPS FOR THE MELAMINE

1. With an old paintbrush, apply a thin coat of the Wood Creation product. To imitate wood grain, maintain the same directional movement throughout the application process. Allow it to dry for approximately three hours.

2. Once the surface is completely dry to the touch, apply one coat of the walnut colour stain with a staining cloth. Wipe any excess, and do so in the same direction as with the base coat application.

3. With a polyester-bristle paintbrush, apply two coats of a water-based varnish, which will render the surface washable and stain resistant. Take care to sand lightly with 400-grit sandpaper between each coat. Wipe with a clean cloth.

## A BIODEGRADABLE DEGREASER

A new product on the market, TSPe is an organic, phosphate-free degreasing agent. It performs as well as the traditional T.S.P. but without the harmful side effects. Easy to use, this product does not require rinsing after application. It saves time and does not damage the surface. You can clean bare wood without risking discoloration. TSPe is biodegradable and does not pollute waterways or septic tanks.

## CUTTING TOOLS

Melamine is a brittle material that is difficult to cut because it can chip easily. It is therefore necessary to use a very sharp, thin blade. Equipped with numerous teeth, the blade of a circular or table saw, once adapted for slicing through melamine or laminate, allows you to make clean cuts.

*The use of diagonal lines highlights the design's originality. Draw some inspiration from this personal touch for your own creations.*

# Remodelled dressers

To think these five dressers could easily have been relegated to the attic! And yet, all that was needed to achieve these spectacular results was a combination of woodworking savvy, creative thinking and constructive efforts. Scottish plaids, lustrous lacquers and furry drawers have gone beyond rejuvenating these furnishings; they have resulted in a transformation guaranteed to electrify any décor. This goes to prove that creativity knows no bounds!

**BEFORE**

*Surprise! A plain white melamine dresser was the starting point for this impressive transformation.*

*Although the bedroom is primarily used for sleeping, that doesn't mean we should neglect its appearance. Falling asleep and waking up are so much more pleasant when they occur in beautiful surroundings. This piece of furniture has undergone a major transformation through the versatile use of mouldings and handles. The tall dresser, angled in a corner of the room, is crowned with a cornice, giving it added volume. A rich colour treatment accentuates its luxurious elegance.*

RESEARCH: NATHALIE JOLICŒUR. STYLING: GUYLAINE ST-AMAND. PHOTOGRAPHY: MARTIN HOUDE, PRATICO MEDIA.

# FROM ONE ERA TO ANOTHER

**T**his dresser's appearance has caught up with the times. There's no trace of the sixties left! Its straight lines, stainless steel handles and dark colours are in keeping with today's trends.

RESEARCH: NATHALIE JOLICŒUR. STYLING: LOUISE BOUCHARD. PHOTOGRAPHY: MARTIN HOUDE, PRATICO MEDIA.

*Required material:* stripping product, 100-grit, 120-grit, 150-grit and 320-grit sandpaper; Richelieu (brand name) handles #26217195 and #2537024195.

*Finish:* Chemcraft International (brand name) stain #CHM-9244; Wood Kote (brand name) Ultra Poly Kote (polyurethane) varnish with silk finish.

*Required tools:* jigsaw, lead pencil, measuring tape, latex gloves, stripping gloves, wooden scraper, clean cloth, old paintbrush, steel wool, resin cloth, staining cloth, paintbrush with 100% natural-silk bristles.

### Step-by-step instructions:

- ✔ Remove the toe-kick with a jigsaw.
- ✔ Strip the dresser (see steps on pages 7 and 8).
- ✔ Apply the stain and varnish to the dresser (see steps on pages 9, 10 and 11).
- ✔ Install the new handles.

*The new finish exudes inviting warmth. The clean lines of the stylish handles fit marvellously with the dresser's new design.*

## BEFORE

*Isn't it surprising to see the extent of the impact that a colour change and new hardware can have on furniture?*

## MY FAVOURITE IDEA

**T**o create the illusion that the dresser is standing on legs, the area at the bottom was carved using a jigsaw. This results in a more contemporary look.

# CONVENTIONAL SPIRIT

**S**erving as a nightstand, this small dresser is remarkably simple in nature. Created with mouldings, the framed panels at the front add stylish texture. The use of colour inside the moulding's groove is subtle but effective. Elegantly curved handles contrast beautifully with the overall linear design. RESEARCH AND STYLING: NATHALIE JOLICŒUR. PHOTOGRAPHY: MARTIN HOUDE, PRATICO MEDIA.

*Required material: oil-based primer, Etchemin (brand name) decorative mouldings #09316, wood filler; all-purpose glue; Richelieu (brand name) handles #10496900; T.S.P. or TSPe; 120-grit and 600-grit sandpaper; finishing nails.*

*Finish: Para (brand name) oil-based paint #P667-4 (for the dresser) and #P657-3 (for the mouldings); oil-based varnish.*

*Required tools: mitre saw; air-powered nail gun or hammer; drill; lead pencil; measuring tape; paintbrush; clean cloth, paintbrush with 100% natural-silk bristles.*

*Step-by-step instructions:*

- ✔ *Prepare the melamine surface (see steps on page 14).*
- ✔ *Proceed with the finishing steps for the dresser (see steps below).*
- ✔ *Install the new handles.*

**BEFORE**

*Initially, this piece of furniture resembled a filing cabinet. It did, however, have the potential to become a charming addition to the bedroom.*

## FINISHING STEPS FOR THE DRESSER

1. *Measure the face of the drawers. Use a mitre saw to cut mouldings #09316 to size. Apply all-purpose glue to the moulding pieces and affix to the drawers, 1¹/₂" from the edge. Secure with ⁵/₈" finishing nails. Fill the holes and joints with wood filler.*

2. *Apply one coat of primer to the entire dresser. For the base colour, apply two coats of colour #P667-4, using a paintbrush with 100% natural-silk bristles. Allow it to dry between coats, as per the manufacturer's instructions. For the finish, mix three parts oil-based varnish with one part colour #P657-3 and apply to the grooves of the mouldings.*

3. *Wipe the excess paint with a clean cloth until you obtain the desired finish. Then, apply two to three coats of varnish to better protect the finish. Sand with 600-grit sandpaper between each coat. Wipe the dust off with a clean cloth.*

# SCOTTISH PLAID

**D**isguised as a kilt, the dresser is simply adorable! This represents an original utilization of an otherwise traditional print. Scottish plaid is famous for having withstood the test of time. It's impressive to see how this forever-fashionable print can dress up a room. Long live these oh-so-Scottish squares!

*Required material:* oil-based primer; T.S.P. or TSPe; 120-grit sandpaper.

*Finish:* Sico (brand name) latex paint #6097-32 (yellow), #6051-75 (red) and #6140-63 (green).

*Required tools:* measuring tape; carpenter's square; lead pencil; 1/2" flat paintbrush; paintbrush with 100% natural-silk bristles; foam roller; polyester-bristle paintbrush; masking tape.

*Step-by-step instructions:*

✔ Prepare the melamine surface (see steps on page 14).

✔ Apply two coats of colour #6097-32 to the dresser with a polyester-bristle paintbrush.

✔ Proceed with the finishing steps for the dresser (see steps below).

*This type of dresser can be found in most used furniture stores. Hurry: you can probably get one now at a ridiculously low price!*

BEFORE

## FINISHING STEPS FOR THE DRESSER

*1 Once the surface is dry, use a carpenter's square to trace the outline of the squares that will be painted red.*

*2 Put masking tape along all of the traced lines. To keep the paint from seeping through, make sure that the tape has adhered well to the surface.*

*3 With a foam roller, apply colour #6051-75. Apply the number of coats necessary to ensure that the resulting colour is completely opaque.*

*What charming results! Who could resist this plaid motif? Now it's your turn to select your colours and pick up the masking tape.*

*4 Remove the masking tape before the last coat is completely dry.*

*5 Once the surface is dry, trace the lines for the areas that will be painted green. Affix masking tape along the exterior of the traced lines. With a flat paint-brush, apply colour #6140-63, and again, apply the number of coats needed until the colour is completely opaque. Remove the masking tape before the last coat is completely dry.*

RESEARCH: NATHALIE JOLICŒUR. STYLING: GUYLAINE ST-AMAND. PHOTOGRAPHY: MARTIN HOUDE, PRATICO MEDIA.

# ANIMAL ACT

These days, fur is regularly found in fashionable designs. The fake fur that adorns this dresser makes it the room's focal point. Each drawer, boasting its own personality and texture, is eye-catching. The designer could have opted for real fur, which is readily available in used clothing stores. But imitation fur also allows you to reach your goal, which is to design an extravagantly original creation.

BEFORE

*To say the least, this piece of furniture has gone beyond the ordinary. This new jungle look has succeeded in erasing all evidence of any youthful innocence.*

RESEARCH: NATHALIE JOLICŒUR. STYLING: GUYLAINE ST-AMAND. PHOTO: MARTIN HOUDE, PRATICO MEDIA.

## FINISHING STEPS FOR THE DRESSER

*Required material:* oil-based primer; T.S.P. or TSPe; 120-grit sandpaper; QCL, Quinko-Tek (brand name) handles #1036A01; fabrics of your choice; glue or adhesive specially formulated for the chosen fabrics.

*Finish:* Sico (brand name) paint #6068-83 (for the base coat) and DecoArt Americana (brand name) Traditional Burnt Umber (for the leather faux finish); latex varnish.

*Required tools:* measuring tape; lead pencil; 10-mm paint roller; hair dryer; polyester-bristle paintbrush; ³/4" flat paintbrush; staining cloth; clean cloth; scissors; latex gloves.

*Step-by-step instructions:*

✔ Prepare the melamine surface (see steps on page 14).

✔ With a roller, apply a thick, uniform and opaque coat of colour #6068-83 to the dresser, except for the face of the drawers.

✔ Proceed with the finishing steps for the dresser (see steps to the right).

✔ Install the new handles.

1 To create a leather texture, use a 10-mm roller and apply a thick coat of latex varnish. Work on small areas of 1 square foot at a time.

2 When varnish dries quickly, a crackled effect results. Therefore, immediately dry the varnish applied with a hair dryer, ensuring to direct the heat close to the surface. The heat and speed should both be on the maximum setting so that the varnish crackles everywhere. Repeat the operation on all sides of the dresser.

3 With a flat ³/4" paintbrush, randomly apply the Traditional Burnt Umber paint.

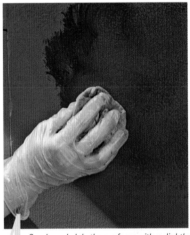

4 Scrub and dab the surface with a lightly damp cloth so that the cracks and grooves will be left looking darker. Keep the raised areas lighter and allow the orange-skin texture to show. If needed, repeat the operation in the areas that are too light until you obtain the desired effect. Then, apply one coat of varnish with a polyester-bristle paintbrush.

*A leather faux finish was applied to counterbalance the weighty feel of the fake fur. The two textures coexist in perfect harmony.*

5 Measure the face of the drawers and cut your fabric or fur pieces to size. Use the type of glue that corresponds to your chosen fabric. Note that all-purpose white glue is convenient for thick fabric such as fur. As for thinner fabric, keep in mind that liquid glue could go through the fabric and stain it. Consider the use of double-sided adhesive tape or spray glue specifically made for fabric.

# Reinventing three tables

One should always make an attempt to find beauty within the ordinary.

An outdated look can still throw off a spark that will light up

your imagination. Clean lines often conceal

a world of possibilities. Here, creativity knows

no bounds as it conjures up three

exquisitely original table designs. Through

the magic of paint, ceramic tiles and veneer,

they become unrecognizable. Without a

doubt, these masterpieces will whet your decorative appetite!

The long day is over     The long day is over     The long day is over

# HOME COMFORT

*No matter from which angle you examine this table, it is indeed difficult to detect any charm. Despite that fact, creative ingenuity has prevailed!*

**T**his pier table creates a romantic setting for an intimate tête-à-tête. From the very first glance, the elegant script invites occupants to sit back and relax. The contrasting overlays of light grey, charcoal grey and red add an undeniably unique touch.

RESEARCH: NATHALIE JOLICŒUR. STYLING: GUYLAINE ST-AMAND.
PHOTOGRAPHY: MARTIN HOUDE, PRATICO MEDIA

*Required material:* oil-based primer; T.S.P. or TSPe; 120-grit sandpaper; stencil design; stencil plastic to create stencils; repositionable spray adhesive for stencils.

*Finish:* Para (brand name) latex paint #P2268-4 (light grey), #P2271-5 (dark grey) and #P378-8 (red); water-based varnish.

*Required tools:* measuring tape; utility knife with a thin blade; carpenter's square; lead pencil; fine point black marker; paintbrush and foam roller; paintbrush with 100% natural-silk bristles; polyester-bristle paintbrush; masking tape.

*Step-by-step instructions:*

- ✔ *Prepare the melamine surface (see steps on page 14).*

- ✔ *Use a lead pencil and a carpenter's square to trace the outline of the areas to be painted. Affix masking tape to the exterior part of those areas. Press firmly on the tape to ensure that it adheres well to the surface.*

- ✔ *With a foam roller, apply two coats of colour #P2268-4 and #P2271-5 inside the respective areas. Remove the masking tape before the second coat dries completely.*

- ✔ *Create the stencil (see steps to the right).*

- ✔ *Proceed with the finishing steps for the table (see steps below).*

## CREATING THE STENCIL

**1** Use your computer to create your stencil pattern and print it. Using a photocopier, enlarge the pattern to the desired size. Position a sheet of stencil plastic onto the pattern. Trace the exterior lines with a fine point black marker.

**2** To prevent errors and end up cutting parts of letters that should remain, trace a few guiding marks. When you are ready to start cutting, these marks will serve as tie-down guides. To cut the contour of the letters, use a utility knife with a very thin and flexible blade.

*The stylish lettering would lead us to think that someone's graceful handwriting came into play. But no! Such elegance was actually bestowed through stencilling.*

## FINISHING STEPS FOR THE TABLE

Apply a light coat of spray adhesive to the back of the stencil. Wait a few minutes before positioning the stencil on the table, in the area where you wish to write the phrase. Use a clean, dry cloth and press down on the stencil until it adheres to the surface. **1**

**2** Dip a foam paintbrush lightly into the paint and apply it to the stencil, dabbing vertically. As such, there is less risk of the paint seeping through the stencil. Make sure to cover the entire surface evenly. Protect your work by applying two coats of water-based varnish with a polyester-bristle paintbrush.

# INSPIRED BY GAUDI

It's like being in Barcelona and admiring Gaudi's magnificent architectural masterpieces and mosaics. Opting for such an interesting mosaic tile arrangement was a great idea. This type of originality is what confers the sought-after distinctive style of recycled furniture. The lizard seems to be basking in the sun!

*This bird's-eye view allows us to see all of the design elements. The primary colours create beautiful contrasts and the new reddish colour applied to the wood was definitely a sound choice.*

**RESEARCH:** NATHALIE JOLICŒUR. **STYLING:** GUYLAINE ST-AMAND. **PHOTOGRAPHY:** MARTIN HOUDE, PRATICO MEDIA.

*Required material:* oil-based primer; 80-grit and 120-grit sandpaper; pine decorative moulding; wood filler; ceramic tiles of various colours; premixed mortar; premixed grout; masking tape; nails.

*Finish:* Sico (brand name) paint #6057-85.

*Required tools:* latex gloves; lead pencil; measuring tape; mitre saw; hammer; tile cutter; small trowel; grout float; grout sponge.

*Step-by-step instructions:*

- ✓ Sand the table lightly with 80-grit sandpaper. Continue with 120-grit sandpaper.
- ✓ Sketch the desired drawing on the table.
- ✓ Cut the decorative moulding to size and affix it around the edge of the tabletop with finishing nails. Fill the nail holes with wood filler. Allow it to dry and sand lightly.
- ✓ Proceed with the finishing steps for the table (see steps to the right).
- ✓ Protect the mosaic design with masking tape.
- ✓ Apply one coat of oil-based primer to the table, followed by two coats of colour #6057-85. Remember to respect the recommended drying time between each coat.

## FINISHING STEPS FOR THE TABLE

1 *To break the tiles, place them inside a cloth and hit them with a hammer. This way, the pieces will be uneven.*

2 *Place the ceramic pieces according to the sketch drawn on the table. Since the pieces are not yet glued, you can move them around as often as you wish.*

## BEFORE

*The table's impressive structure was ideally suited for this mosaic. A more fragile table would appear vulnerable under the weight of the tiles.*

3 *Use a tile cutter to modify the shape of the pieces that do not fit in well with the mosaic design.*

4 *Once you have reproduced your sketch entirely, remove and glue the pieces one by one with the premixed mortar.*

5 *When the mortar has set, spread the grout, making sure to fill all of the joints. Wipe the grout with a sponge specifically designed for this purpose. Rinse several times to eliminate any residue.*

# NEW CHIC

**S**urprisingly, you can obtain stunning results when applying a laminate! Here, the fresh-looking finish conveys a contemporary style, and only a few hours were needed to achieve this look.

RESEARCH: NATHALIE JOLICŒUR. STYLING: GUYLAINE ST-AMAND. PHOTOGRAPHY: MARTIN HOUDE, PRATICO MEDIA.

*This melamine table has acquired breathtaking elegance.*

BEFORE

*Required material:* Formica (brand name) laminate #6944-58; contact glue; Richelieu (brand name) table legs #61271010; T.S.P. or TSPe; 120-grit sandpaper.

*Required tools:* table saw and Formica knife; ruler; drill; router equipped with a ball-bearing straight bit; foam roller; cloth; veneer roller; medium-size serrated file.

*Step-by-step instructions:*

- ✔ Remove the table legs.
- ✔ Prepare the melamine surface (see steps on page 14).
- ✔ Proceed with the finishing steps for the table (see steps below).
- ✔ Install the new legs.

*Fine metallic grey lines weave an attractive pattern. Nothing more than this was required to revitalize the table.*

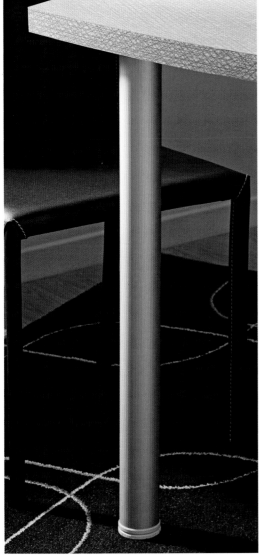

*Obviously, the transformation would only be complete once the table legs were replaced. Now they match the laminate's colour scheme.*

## FINISHING STEPS FOR THE TABLE

**1** Measure the perimeter of the table, the width of the edge and the surface of the table. With a ruler and a Formica knife, cut the Formica laminate to size. You can also use a table saw to cut the straight lines.

**2** With a foam roller, apply contact glue to the back of the Formica strips and to the edge of the table. As usual, remember to respect the recommended drying time. Affix the trim to the edge and use a veneer roller to eliminate the air bubbles.

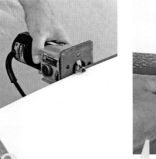

**3** Cut the excess Formica laminate with a router equipped with a ball-bearing straight bit.

**4** File the corners to remove the excess. You must also file the junction between the edge and the top to ensure a smooth surface.

**5** Apply contact glue to the back of the tabletop laminate piece as well as to the tabletop itself. Position the piece of Formica laminate on the table and allow for the recommended drying time. Use a veneer roller to remove the air bubbles. Repeat steps 3 and 4 to complete the project.

# Four chairs, four styles

Frequently used and very utilitarian, chairs are often overlooked when it comes to updating one's décor. In reality, chairs are the perfect starting point for those who wish to practice and perfect different decorative techniques without spending a fortune. Giving them some pizzazz need not be a complicated proposition. So hurry up and go scour used furniture stores to find this work of art that could soon become a source of pride.

BEFORE

*A closer look at these seemingly haphazard creations reveals traces of bygone school days.*

*This springtime look conjures up the countryside where nature abounds with greenery.*

RESEARCH: NATHALIE JOLICŒUR. STYLING: GUYLAINE ST-AMAND. PHOTOGRAPHY: MARTIN HOUDE, PRATICO MEDIA

# REFRESHING

The décor is so fresh; you'd swear you were about to settle down on the grass for a picnic lunch. This charming assortment of scrapbooking paper offers endless decorating possibilities. Not only is it lovely, but the finish on this paper is extremely resistant. Sitting on it presents no problem.

*Whoever said stripes and polka dots don't get along was sadly mistaken. Do dare to mix and match different motifs!*

*Here, stripes have the starring role! This close-up shows how well the paper flawlessly adheres to all the surfaces.*

## FINISHING STEPS FOR THE CHAIR

This example is a tribute to patchwork. It looks as though one of grandma's cushions was sewn to the chair's seat.

**Required material:** oil-based spray primer; 80-grit and 120-grit sandpaper; scrapbooking decorative paper; acrylic medium with matte finish.

**Finish:** Benjamin Moore (brand name) paint #OC-84 (beige), #HC-37 (brown) and #2147-40 (green).

**Required tools:** carpenter's square; lead pencil; utility knife with a thin blade; plastic putty knife; polyester-bristle paintbrush.

**Step-by-step instructions:**

- ✔ Sand the surface lightly with 80-grit sandpaper. Continue with 120-grit sandpaper. Apply one coat of oil-based spray primer.
- ✔ Apply two coats of paint to the chairs. For a more creative look, alternate the colours on the leg braces and on the legs. Use the pictures to spark your imagination.
- ✔ Proceed with the finishing steps for the chair (see steps to the right).

1. Cut the decorative paper into strips. To mark the edges of the seat, place the paper on the seat and use a carpenter's square that facilitates marking on a hard surface. With a lead pencil, draw a line on the back of the paper to mark the edges.

2. To ensure that the strips do not wrinkle at the time of installation, cut the overlapping portion of the paper into thin strips as shown.

3. Apply one coat of medium with matte finish to the surface to be decorated. Lay the paper down, taking care not to form bubbles. Smooth out the paper with a small plastic trowel. Apply one coat of medium with matte finish directly to the paper.

4. Repeat this step around all side edges, working with small sections at a time. This will avoid tearing the strips.

5. Repeat these same steps to cover the back of the chair.

# COMFORT ZONE

**A**ll bundled up in fabric, these chairs appear to be very comfy. This concept serves to encourage experimentation with printed fabric. Alternating matching prints on each of the chairs will infuse energy and liven up your décor. It's important to remember that the print style selected will impact on the design's style.

*Required material:* latex primer; 80-grit and 120-grit sandpaper; fabric; thread and needle.

*Finish:* Sico (brand name) paint #6051-71 (red) and #6141-63 (apple green).

*Required tools:* sewing machine; measuring tape; polyester-bristle paintbrush; white pencil for fabric.

*Step-by-step instructions:*

✔ *Sand the chairs lightly with 80-grit sandpaper. Continue with 120-grit sandpaper. Apply one coat of latex primer.*

✔ *Paint one chair red and the other apple green, applying two coats of paint to each.*

✔ *Proceed with the finishing steps for the chair (see steps below).*

✔ *Attach the fabric to the seat of the chair and insert the piece of fabric onto the back of the chair.*

*This is the style of chair that's hidden beneath this elegant fabric. Its straight lines were very well-suited to the design.*

## FINISHING STEPS FOR THE CHAIR

*Measure the seat of the chair. Cut the #1 piece of fabric, adding an allowance of ⁵/₈" for the seams. Do the same for the sides, the front and the back, according to the plan below. Cut a strip of fabric 1" x 68" to serve as a rim around the seat. Place a rope inside this strip of fabric, fold the fabric in two and sew it along its entire length. Affix the rim all the way around the seat portion with pins, attaching the #2, #3, #4 and #5 panels along with it. Sew the necessary seams to attach one piece to another.*

*To make the tiebacks, cut two strips of fabric 1" wide x 8" long. Fold the width of each strip into three. Make a seam in the centre. Fold the tiebacks in two and affix them to the back end of the seat piece with a seam on each outside corner.*

*To make the cover for the back of the chair, measure the width at the top end, and measure the width one foot lower down. Many chairs do not have a perfectly straight back. For the height, measure a one-foot length. Cut two pieces of fabric, adding a ⁵/₈" allowance for the seam. Sew the two pieces together matching the outside of the fabric from one piece to another. Turn the completed cover inside out.*

*The delicate floral print has a sweet countrified appeal. The chair was repainted to match the fabric.*

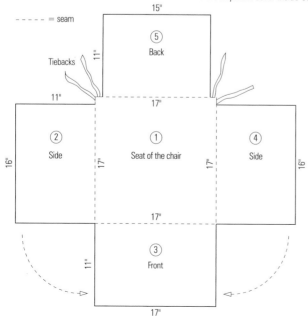

- - - - = seam

15"

⑤ Back

11"

Tiebacks

11"     17"

② Side     ① Seat of the chair     ④ Side

16"     17"          17"          16"

17"

③ Front

11"

17"

RESEARCH: NATHALIE JOLICŒUR. STYLING: GUYLAINE ST-AMAND. PHOTOGRAPHY: MARTIN HOUDE, PRATICO MEDIA.

# BACK-TO-SCHOOL

**T**he argyle print preserves the academic character of this wooden chair. Clad
in a diamond-print vest, the chair reclaims its youthful appearance. Such a creation
can spice up the décor in any child's room or occupy an area reserved for homework.
The colour combination corresponds to the shades available on the usual paint colour
charts. As you can imagine, the possibilities are endless!

RESEARCH: NATHALIE JOLICŒUR. STYLING: GUYLAINE ST-AMAND. PHOTOGRAPHY: MARTIN HOUDE, PRATICO MEDIA.

This close-up helps illustrate all the pattern details, which should help you in designing your own argyle print.

If there is one type of chair that is readily available in most furniture stores, this is the one.

**BEFORE**

**Required material:** *latex primer; T.S.P. or TSPe; 80-grit and 120-grit sandpaper; cellulose sponge; cork cap; finishing nails; sheet of paper; hot glue.*

**Finish:** *Sico (brand name) paint #6152-53 (for the chair); DecoArt Americana (brand name) paint: Traditional Burnt Umber, Sky Blue, Light Green and White (for the diamond shapes); water-based varnish.*

**Required tools:** *hot glue gun; plastic container; measuring tape; kitchen knife or utility knife; polyester-bristle paintbrush; fine point black marker.*

**Step-by-step instructions:**

✔ *Clean the surface with T.S.P. or TSPe. Sand the chair lightly with 80-grit sandpaper. Continue with 120-grit sandpaper. Apply one coat of latex primer.*

✔ *Apply two coats of colour #6152-53 to the chair.*

✔ *Create the stencil (see steps below).*

✔ *Proceed with the finishing steps for the chair (see steps to the right).*

## FINISHING STEPS FOR THE CHAIR

1 *Dip the stencil into the paint.*

2 *Position the stencil in the centre, on the back piece of the chair.*

## CREATING THE STENCIL

1 *Cut a diamond shape from a sheet of paper. Trace the pattern on a cellulose sponge with a fine point black marker. Cut the sponge with a kitchen knife or a utility knife. Do not dispose of the remnants, as they will be useful later on.*

2 *To facilitate the handling of the stencil, affix the cork cap to the back of the stencil (sponge) with hot glue.*

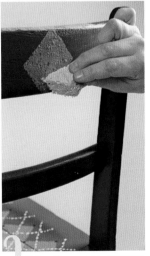

3 *Using the sponge remnants, touch up the paint job. Alternate the colours of the diamond shapes and allow it to dry.*

4 *Dip the head of a nail into paint and create the white and brown stitch pattern, referring to the design on the picture as an example. Apply two coats of varnish for better protection.*

# MOULIN ROUGE

**W**ow! This stunning chair belongs in the dressing room of a Moulin Rouge cabaret star. Feathers, pearls, jewels and satin infuse glamour into this design. A metallic finish accentuates the elegance. Such a creation would seduce any artistic soul as well as any admirer of exceptional aesthetic designs. RESEARCH: NATHALIE JOLICŒUR. STYLING: GUYLAINE ST-AMAND. PHOTOGRAPHY: MARTIN HOUDE, PRATICO MEDIA.

## BEFORE

*This spectacular transformation was doubtlessly inspired by the chair's graceful curves.*

**Required material:** *oil-based spray primer; 80-grit and 120-grit sandpaper; hot glue; fabric glue; two different types of feather fringe; #4 carpet tacks; metal wire; three peacock feathers; quilt stuffing; black satin; decorative ribbon.*

**Finish:** *spray paint with instant chrome finish.*

**Required tools:** *stapler and staples; hot glue gun; hammer; scissors.*

**Step-by-step instructions:**

- ✔ *Remove the seat from the chair.*
- ✔ *Sand the chair lightly with 80-grit sandpaper. Continue with 120-grit sandpaper. Apply one coat of oil-based spray primer.*
- ✔ *Proceed with the finishing steps for the chair (see steps to the right).*
- ✔ *With the hot glue gun, affix the peacock feathers to the back of the chair, in the centre.*
- ✔ *Conceal the lower portion of the feathers with a black pearl necklace, securing it with hot glue.*

*By itself, the peacock feather was already quite ravishing. Adorning it with jewellery enhanced its beauty. Each tiny detail serves to heighten the coquettish appeal.*

## FINISHING STEPS FOR THE CHAIR

1 *Apply two coats of spray paint with instant chrome finish to the chair.*

2 *While it is drying, cover the seat with a piece of quilt stuffing to give it height. Cover it with black satin and staple the fabric under the seat, all the way around.*

3 *Cut two strips of feather fringe of different types. At the bottom of one of the strips, apply a bead of fabric glue.*

*Decidedly, this chair is gorgeous, head-to-toe, especially with those pretty ribbons wrapped around its legs.*

4 *Affix a metal wire and attach the other type of feather fringe on the bead of glue. This will prevent the strips of fringe from drooping. Prepare a second band of fringes by repeating these steps.*

5 *To affix the strips of fringe to each side of the chair, use #4 carpet tacks.*

# One model, three armoires

BEFORE

*This is the piece of furniture we are referring to. Inexpensive and easy to find, this armoire is not difficult to transform. You are limited only by your budget and your imagination.*

Find out how one armoire can be magically transformed into three distinct creations that can meet the needs of a young girl, her parents and her brother. When restoring items, one learns that even the most insignificant pieces merit attention. Plain old furniture can suddenly become perfectly suited to a particular project. Even a run-of-the-mill melamine armoire can inspire a successful metamorphosis.

Here's the proof.

# PRETTY IN PINK

This armoire's soft hues and refined detailing exude calm. Designed to help avoid a messy room, the shelf dividers create practical compartments for sorting various accessories. The rattan baskets are ideal for storing those tiny collectibles that children so adore. The open shelf at the top imparts an airy feel to the armoire.

RESEARCH: NATHALIE JOLICŒUR. STYLING: GUYLAINE ST-AMAND. PHOTOGRAPHY: MARTIN HOUDE, PRATICO MEDIA.

**Required material:** ³/4-inch-thick MDF board (for the shelf dividers, the top of the armoire and the toe-kick); Richelieu (brand name) handles #70355085; primer; T.S.P. or TSPe; 120-grit sandpaper; all-purpose glue; nails and screws.

**Alexandria (brand name) mouldings:** #CR694-9U (top of the armoire) and #00612-30 (decorative panel frames).

**Finish:** Behr (brand name) paint #W-B-420 with satin finish (cream) and #100B-4 with satin finish (pink); Saman (brand name) stain #204 (for the top of the armoire).

**Required tools:** mitre saw; table saw; jigsaw; drill; wood bit or 1" Forstner bit; measuring tape; utility knife; level; lead pencil; trim paintbrush; 4" foam roller.

**Step-by-step instructions:**

- Remove the doors, handles and shelves. Cut the top of the doors to the length required so that the top shelf is exposed.
- Prepare the melamine surface (see steps on page 14).
- Cut moulding #CR694-9U and affix it to the top of the armoire with finishing nails.
- Proceed with the finishing steps for the doors (see steps below).

- Trace the toe-kick pattern onto the MDF board and cut it out with a jigsaw. Place the blade of the table saw at a 45° angle and cut the top part of the toe-kick to create a ¹/4" bevel. Cut a 45° angle at the ends and affix the pieces to the bottom of the armoire with finishing nails.
- Measure the distance between the shelves. Refer to the plan for the dividers and enlarge it to fit between the shelves, according to your measurements. Trace the pattern onto the MDF board and cut it out with a jigsaw.
- Paint the inside of the armoire, the shelves and the dividers with colour #100B-4. Do not paint the contour of the shelves, the back end of the dividers or underneath them. The extra layer created by a coat of paint could hinder the smooth insertion of the pieces. Allow it to dry for approximately 48 hours before installing the shelves and the dividers inside the armoire. Use finishing nails to secure the dividers.
- Paint the exterior of the armoire, the top moulding and the toe-kick with colour #W-S-420.
- Cut a piece of MDF board for the top of the armoire and stain it with colour #204. Once dry, affix it to the top of the armoire. The piece of MDF must be cut and positioned so that it extends ¹/2" over the sides and the front.
- Stain the handles with colour #204 before installing them on the doors.

## FINISHING STEPS FOR THE DOORS

Measure the doors. With a mitre saw, cut moulding #00612-30 to size. Apply all-purpose glue to the mouldings and affix them to the doors and to the sides of the armoire, 1¹/2" from the edge. Refer to the photo to visualize the installation. Reinforce with ⁵/8" finishing nails. Fill the holes and joints with wood filler.

Place the decorative pattern in the centre of the frame created with mouldings. Hammer a nail into the centre of each circle to serve as your guideline for cutting.

Remove the pattern. With a wood bit or Forstner bit, drill three holes. Then, cut out the stem with a jigsaw.

*The divider added to the open top section shows that attention to detail was important. Its beautiful design is remarkable.*

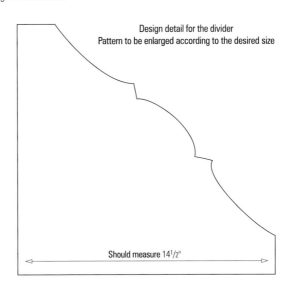

Design detail for the divider
Pattern to be enlarged according to the desired size

Should measure 14$^1$/$_2$"

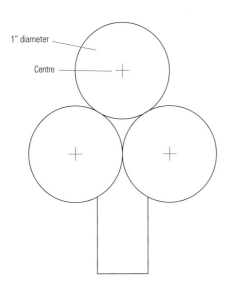

1" diameter

Centre

Pattern detail for the door
Actual size of the pattern to be drilled

*Yes, mouldings are often used. And colour schemes are often taken into account. But cut-outs like the ones that were made on these door panels are definitely in a class of their own.*

*Incorporating a carved MDF toe-kick into the design offers yet another touch of elegance.*

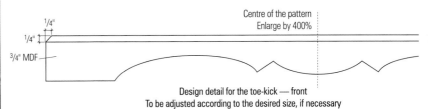

1/4"
1/4"
3/4" MDF

Centre of the pattern
Enlarge by 400%

Design detail for the toe-kick — front
To be adjusted according to the desired size, if necessary

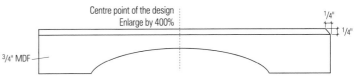

Centre point of the design
Enlarge by 400%

1/4"
1/4"
3/4" MDF

Design detail for the toe-kick – side
To be adjusted according to the desired size, if necessary

# FOR TIGHT SPACES

In small areas, getting the most out of the available space is important. At first sight, this appears to be a regular storage cabinet, which adds decorative value to the room. However, once the armoire's doors open, its well-kept secret is revealed.

*Required material:* MDF board, $^1/_4$" thick (for the mouldings), MDF board, $^3/_4$" thick (for the piece at the top of the armoire and the toe-kick); Richelieu (brand name) handles #550961-64 and full overlay hinges; 100% acrylic primer; T.S.P. or TSPe; 120-grit sandpaper; all-purpose glue; nails and screws.

*Finish:* Behr (brand name) paint with semi-gloss finish #750B-7; Blue Mountain (brand name) wallpaper from the Cross Current catalogue (optional).

*Required tools:* mitre saw; table saw; drill; measuring tape; utility knife; level; lead pencil; foam paintbrush; 4" foam roller.

*Step-by-step instructions:*

✔ *Remove the doors, handles and shelves.*

✔ *Prepare the melamine surface (see steps on page 14).*

✔ *Proceed with the finishing steps for the armoire (see steps below).*

✔ *Paint the shelves, as well as the exterior and interior of the armoire with colour #750B-7, except for the back panel. Do not paint the contour of the shelves. The extra layer created by a coat of paint could hinder the smooth insertion of the shelving. Allow the shelves to dry for approximately 48 hours before installing them. Install the wallpaper on the back panel of the armoire before inserting the shelves.*

✔ *Cut and affix the MDF board to the top of the armoire. This piece must be cut and positioned so that it extends by $^1/_2$" over the sides and the front.*

✔ *Measure and cut the pieces forming the toe-kick. Place the table saw at a 45° angle and cut the top part of the toe-kick to create a $^1/_4$" bevel. Cut a 45° angle at the ends and affix the pieces to the bottom of the armoire with finishing nails.*

✔ *Install the handles on the doors and the new hinges.*

## INSTALLING WALLPAPER

Remove the back panel of the armoire. Measure the surface to be covered and add an extra inch to allow for error. Cut the first strip with a straight-edge guide and a utility knife. Roll the cut strip and immerse it in a water tray for ten seconds. Fold the wallpaper like an accordion, glue side against glue side, and let sit for five minutes. Install the strip starting at the top of the panel. Slide the smoothing brush from top to bottom and from the centre towards the sides. Cut excess with a utility knife and a straight-edge guide. Wipe the surface with a clean cloth. If it is necessary to use two widths of wallpaper, follow the same steps, making sure to match the pattern along the seam.

## FINISHING STEPS FOR THE ARMOIRE

*The distinctive lines created by mouldings convey character to this piece of furniture. This armoire could stand proudly in any room of the house, whether in the living room, kitchen, den, dining room or bedroom.*

1 *Measure the doors and cut the $^1/_4$" MDF into 2$^1/_2$-inch-wide strips and to the required length. Glue them to the door panels and to the sides of the armoire. Add finishing nails to secure the strips. Refer to the picture for the correct positioning of the strips.*

2 *Once the mouldings have been installed, measure the size of the top square so that you can cut the X-shape pieces that will be placed in the centre. Cut the ends into a V-shape at a 45° angle. Glue the pieces and use finishing nails to secure.*

*You could even pull up a stool to make yourself comfortable. Files and personal items can be stored in decorative storages boxes.*

*Open the doors and see the armoire transform into a desk area where a bulletin board, agenda and pens can be stored. Everything you need to schedule appointments, pay bills or keep your mail is handy. Decorative wallpaper livens up the inside back panel, personalizing the metamorphosis.*

RESEARCH: NATHALIE JOLICŒUR. STYLING: GUYLAINE ST-AMAND. PHOTOGRAPHY: MARTIN HOUDE, PRATICO MEDIA.

# MY SUPERHERO

**T**his armoire was designed to save parents from having to deal with kid-created chaos. Video game joysticks, books, figurines and other valuable objects are safe behind closed doors. The flat door panels are ideal for displaying a poster of your child's favourite superhero. In short, you can create a similarly striking armoire, with Spider-man on guard duty, at minimum cost.

RESEARCH: NATHALIE JOLICŒUR. STYLING: GUYLAINE ST-AMAND. PHOTOGRAPHY: MARTIN HOUDE, PRATICO MEDIA

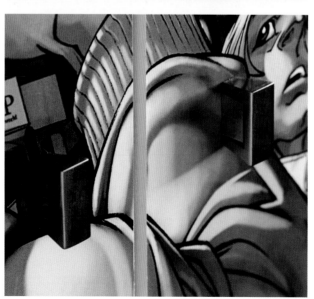

*The door handles are positioned over the poster leaving it intact except for two tiny screw holes.*

*The armoire stands on newly installed metal legs, a detail that extends the high-tech theme to the armoire's exterior.*

*A peek inside reveals a multimedia centre. The metal mouldings placed at the front of the shelves prevent objects from falling in the event that the armoire is accidentally jostled. This practical detailing is also in keeping with the trendy high-tech theme.*

*Required material:* poster; acrylic medium with matte finish; Richelieu (brand name) handles #316323301-95, 20-watt halogen lamp #1002201, 60-watt compact converter #7560; 100% acrylic primer; T.S.P. or TSPe; 120-grit sandpaper; 3/4" x 3/4" 90° aluminium moulding; four stainless steel legs; small metal carpenter's square; nails and screws.

*Finish:* Behr (brand name) paint #370B-7 (yellow) and #560B-7 (blue).

*Required tools:* jigsaw; drill and 1/2" bit; lead pencil; ruler; measuring tape; utility knife; foam paintbrush; 4" foam roller; clean cloth.

*Step-by-step instructions:*

- Remove the doors, handles and shelves.
- Drill a 1/2" hole in the centre and at the top of the armoire to allow access for the halogen lamp's wiring.
- Prepare the melamine surface (see steps on page 14).

- Paint the interior of the armoire and the shelves with colour #370B-7. Paint the inside back panel with colour #560B-7. Do not paint the contour of the shelves. The extra layer created by a coat of paint could hinder the smooth insertion of the pieces. In order to avoid damaging the interior paint, allow the shelves to dry for approximately 48 hours before inserting them back into place.
- Insert the electronic/electrical items in their place. This will allow you to measure and then drill the holes needed for the wiring and for air circulation at the back of the armoire. Reinforce the shelf supporting the television with small metal brackets.
- Lay the armoire on its side and install the legs.
- Affix the aluminium mouldings to the front of the shelves. To do this, use 1/2" screws that you will install from under the shelves. The moulding, being wider than the thickness of the melamine shelves, will create a lip.
- Affix the poster to the doors (see steps below).
- Install the handles and halogen lamp.

## INSTALLING THE POSTER

Place the poster on the armoire. With a ruler, trace a line at the top and the bottom of the poster to indicate the required centre cut. Trace an outline of the poster on the armoire's doors as well, to indicate where to position the poster.

1

2 *Align the ruler on the poster, from top to bottom and as per your traced guidelines. Cut it with a utility knife.*

*A discreet halogen lamp shines on the figurine, highlighting its superhero status.*

3 *Use a foam paintbrush to apply the acrylic medium with matte finish to the back of the first half of the poster.*

4 *Glue the piece onto the door panel, according to your traced guidelines.*

5 *Do the same for the second half of the poster. Once both parts are in place, touch up with glue where necessary. To smooth out the poster, wipe the surface with a clean cloth.*

# One bookcase, three designs

RESEARCH: NATHALIE JOLICŒUR. STYLING: GUYLAINE ST-AMAND. PHOTOGRAPHY: MARTIN HOUDE, PRATICO MEDIA.

*Here come the winds of change! The bookcase is now placed horizontally to attractively occupy the space beneath the window.*

**BEFORE**

*This is a typical bookcase. Many of them are wasting away in basements, long forgotten. After reading this section, take care not to fall as you run down the stairs to retrieve yours!*

What perfectly clean straight lines! Obviously, this piece of furniture is ideal when contemplating a transformation. Once devoid of its plain appearance, this bookcase really perks up a room. This guide will show you how the bookcase starts radiating its new metallic look, how its coquettish nature is captured once dressed up in colourful fabric, and how decorative roll-up blinds serve to camouflage its quieter side. Check it out!

# PERFECT SYMBIOSIS

**H**ere, the owner decided she wanted a serene, Zen-like décor. Mission accomplished! This scene proves that furniture design extends to the environment in which it will evolve. The surrounding décor can contribute to the furniture's rejuvenation and even dictate its appropriateness. This décor expertly complements the bookcase's clean lines.

*The silver leaf overlays confer a distinctive appeal to the bookcase.*

*The diminutive stainless steel legs echo the metallic inserts applied along the top surface of the bookcase.*

*Required material:* oil-based primer; wood filler; six stainless steel legs; T.S.P. or TSPe; 120-grit sandpaper; sheets of silver leaf; adhesive for gold leaf; sealant with satin finish for gold leaf; finishing nails.

*Finish:* Behr (brand name) paint #720F-5.

*Required tools:* table saw; air-powered nail gun or hammer; drill; carpenter's square; lead pencil; measuring tape; ¹/₂" flat paintbrush; 1" shaving brush; foam roller; cheesecloth.

*Step-by-step instructions:*

✓ Transform the shelving unit (see steps below).

✓ Prepare the melamine surface (see steps on page 14).

✓ With a foam roller, apply two coats of colour #720F-5 to the shelving unit.

✓ Proceed with the finishing steps for the shelving unit (see steps below).

## TRANSFORMING THE SHELVING UNIT

1 Remove the screws at the bottom of the shelving unit and take the toe-kick and bottom shelf out.

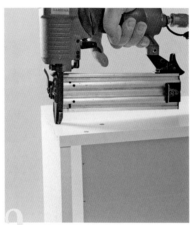

2 Affix that shelf to the bottom of the shelving unit. Turn the unit on its side and install the six legs underneath.

3 Measure the distance between the remaining shelves. Cut two new shelves with a table saw. Install them between the existing shelves, dividing the top and lower compartments into two sections. Use a carpenter's square to guide you.

## FINISHING STEPS FOR THE SHELVING UNIT

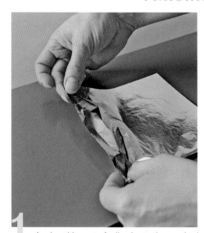

1 Apply a thin coat of adhesive to the required areas, using a flat paintbrush. Wash the paintbrush immediately with soapy water. Allow the adhesive to dry for approximately 60 minutes. It will become transparent as it dries. Take a sheet of silver leaf and place it onto the sticky surface. Make sure that your hands are clean and dry while handling these leaves.

2 Once the surface is covered, slowly smooth out the sheet of silver leaf with a shaving brush. Lightly brush away the excess with the shaving brush.

3 Polish gently with a piece of cheesecloth until the surface is smooth. Apply one coat of sealant with a flat paintbrush.

# CAMOUFLAGE SOLUTION

**A** display of shoes and boots rarely qualifies as an attractive sight. This ingenious designer found a simple but effective solution. In fact, the most complicated part of this project rests in choosing the fabric since fabric stores offer such an amazing selection! The installation process, which involves using self-adhesive Velcro, is quick and easy. As a result, you can vary your décor simply by renewing the fabric. Oversized buttons covered with matching fabric serve as curtain tiebacks. Here we have a perfect pairing of two fabrics.

*Required material:* two different types of fabric; thread and needle; self-adhesive Velcro; coloured string; two large buttons to be fabric-covered.

*Required tools:* measuring tape; scissors; sewing machine.

*Step-by-step instructions:*

✓ To create the fabric panels, measure the height, depth and half the width of the shelving unit. Then, measure the fabric and cut the pieces, adding a seam allowance of $5/8$". Sew the pieces of fabric together, back to back. Sew a hem all around the edge for a better finish.

✓ Install the fabric panels onto the shelving unit (see steps below).

## INSTALLING THE FABRIC PANELS

1. Sew a Velcro strip along the top edge of the panels. Then, glue the other piece of Velcro at the top of the unit. To affix the panels, simply stick the Velcro pieces together.

2. Cover the buttons with fabric and sew them onto the panels, on either side of the shelving unit. To keep the panels open, sew a small string onto each panel. You can then simply hook the string around the buttons.

RESEARCH: NATHALIE JOLICŒUR. STYLING: GUYLAINE ST-AMAND. PHOTOGRAPHY: MARTIN HOUDE, PRATICO MEDIA.

# ON A ROLL!

**R**oll-up blinds don't have to be restricted to window-dressing. Here, they are used to beautify the bookcases. The fabric selection is very important in this case. To create the proper impact, the blinds have to be equally attractive on both sides. That way, when the blinds are rolled up, their decorative value remains. RESEARCH: NATHALIE

JOLICŒUR. STYLING: GUYLAINE ST-AMAND. PHOTOGRAPHY: MARTIN HOUDE, PRATICO MEDIA.

*A cord-operated pulley system is used for rolling and unrolling the blinds. This simple mechanism allows easy access to the contents of the bookcases.*

*Required material (for each blind): 1" x 1" pine strip; fabric with prints on both sides; thread and needle; cardboard roll; coloured string; blind mechanism (sold in fabric stores); small rings; eyelets; Velcro; double-sided adhesive tape for fabric; screws.*

*Required tools: mitre saw; drill; measuring tape; scissors; sewing machine; stapler and staples.*

*Step-by-step instructions:*

- ✔ *Prepare the blind (see steps below).*
- ✔ *Install the blind onto the shelving unit (see following steps).*

## PREPARING THE BLINDS

1 Measure the height and width of the shelving unit. Cut the fabric with a seam allowance of ⁵/₈". For a nicer finish, sew a hem all around the blind. Affix a large cardboard roll, such as those used for fabric and wrapping paper, to the bottom of the blind, using double-sided adhesive tape. Sew the Velcro along the top edge of the blind. The other part of the Velcro will be installed later to the shelving unit itself.

2 At the top of the shelving unit, screw a 1" x 1" pine strip. Install the blind mechanism and the rings to allow easy passage for the string.

3 Install the other part of the Velcro onto the wooden strip with staples. Attaching Velcro to Velcro, install the blind onto the shelving unit.

4 Install the eyelets at the top of the blind; use eyelets of the same size as the rings installed on the pine strip. Thread the string through the eyelets, then through the rings and finally through the blind mechanism. For more details, enquire at the store when purchasing the mechanism.

# New calling

There are no half-measures here, as refurbished furniture undergoes drastic career changes. A coffee table is transformed into a seating arrangement while a dresser becomes a vanity. This section focusses on an entirely new aspect of furniture recycling, where the emphasis rests not only on how it looks but what it does. Do dare to tread off the beaten path!

BEFORE

*This all-metal cabinet sparked this project. Its storage capabilities made it ideal for housing the baby's toiletries and accessories.*

# WILD & CRAZY SIDE

**T**his change table will surely rock the baby's world. The striped and floral motifs are a throwback to the sixties. These vibrant colours, which have replaced the usual pastels, liven up the room without interfering with the peace and quiet that are indispensable in a newborn's nest. This cabinet constitutes an A to Z reinterpretation of what a baby's changing table should resemble.

*Because of the echoing of the colourful motifs, the dressing table is beautiful inside and out. Charming baskets hold the baby clothes and products, keeping things neat and tidy.*

RESEARCH: NATHALIE JOLICŒUR. STYLING: GUYLAINE ST-AMAND.
PHOTOGRAPHY: MARTIN HOUDE, PRATICO MEDIA.

*Required material:* decorative paper; acrylic medium with matte finish; Richelieu (brand name) handles #426140; oil-based primer; T.S.P. or TSPe; 120-grit sandpaper.

*Finish:* Sico (brand name) paint #6147-31 with "Deck and Flooring" finish.

*Required tools:* ruler; lead pencil; measuring tape; scissors; paintbrush; foam roller and foam paintbrush; drill; clean cloth.

*Step-by-step instructions:*

- ✔ Prepare the metal cabinet in the same manner as melamine (see steps on page 14).
- ✔ Apply two coats of colour #6147-31 with a foam roller and a paintbrush.
- ✔ Proceed with the finishing steps for the cabinet (see steps below).
- ✔ Install the new handles.

*The increasing popularity of scrapbooking has lead to the creation of exciting, new paper products. Have fun mixing and matching patterns and colours!*

## FINISHING STEPS FOR THE CABINET

**1** Measure and cut pieces of decorative paper. With a foam paintbrush, apply one coat of medium with matte finish to the back of each piece of paper and glue them onto the cabinet.

**2** To add elegance to your overall design, cut out other motifs as well. Glue the motifs onto the cabinet.

**3** Wait until the collage is dry and apply a few coats of the acrylic medium with matte finish to protect the work. Allow the paper to completely dry between coats to avoid discoloration.

# QUIET CORNER

**T**his beautiful bench, topped with a plush cushion, is an open invitation to relaxation. Furniture like that is so practical, it can occupy a hall entrance and offer support to family and friends as they pull on or take off their footwear.

RESEARCH: NATHALIE JOLICŒUR. STYLING: GUYLAINE ST-AMAND. PHOTOGRAPHY: MARTIN HOUDE, PRATICO MEDIA.

**BEFORE**

*Even a lacquered wood table can be reinvented and transformed into a plush bench.*

*Required material:* T.S.P. or TSPe; acrylic primer; synthetic foam, 2" or 4" thick; quilt stuffing; self-adhesive Velcro; fabric of your choice.

*Finish:* Para (brand name) paint #P2271-5.

*Required tools:* cloth; foam roller; paintbrush; lead pencil; measuring tape; utility knife; scissors; stapler and staples.

*Step-by-step instructions:*

✓ *Clean the table with T.S.P. or TSPe. Apply one coat of acrylic primer with a foam roller and a paintbrush. Let dry.*

✓ *Apply two coats of colour #P2271-5. Allow the required drying time between coats.*

✓ *Measure the top of the table. With a utility knife, cut two pieces from a 2-inch-thick synthetic foam or one 4-inch-thick piece. If you are using two pieces, bind them together with Velcro. Measure and cut the fabric as well as the quilt stuffing, ensuring that there is enough length to reach underneath the base.*

✓ *Proceed with the finishing steps for the bench (see steps below).*

To create a Zen-like atmosphere, an oriental print was selected. It is encouraged to choose a theme for a room, taking care to refrain from going overboard and repeating the theme throughout the entire house.

## FINISHING STEPS FOR THE BENCH

*1* Place the quilt stuffing on the synthetic foam. Cover it completely with the fabric.

*2* Fold the edge of the fabric and staple it on along all sides.

*3* Complete by stapling the corners.

# QUITE HANDY!

**A** dresser is always a welcome addition in a room where assortments of jars, knick knacks, and accessories can be found. In this bathroom, the dresser doubles as a vanity. Its deep drawers, which remain functional, increase the storage capacity. A U-shaped cut-out was made in the centre of the drawers to make allowance for the pipes.

RESEARCH: NATHALIE JOLICŒUR. STYLING: GUYLAINE ST-AMAND. PHOTOGRAPHY: MARTIN HOUDE, PRATICO MEDIA.

*Required material:* stripping product; 100-grit, 120-grit, 150-grit and 320-grit sandpaper.

*Finish:* arts and crafts stain mixture and water-based varnish.

*Required tools:* lead pencil; measuring tape; latex gloves; stripping gloves; wooden scraper; clean cloth; resin cloth; staining cloth; polyester-bristle paintbrush; jigsaw.

*Step-by-step instructions:*

✓ *Strip the dresser completely (see steps on pages 7 and 8).*

✓ *Apply the stain and the varnish to the dresser (see steps on pages 9, 10 and 11).*

✓ *Use the template provided with the sink and trace its outline on top of the dresser. Cut out the shape with a jigsaw.*

✓ *Install the sink, faucets and new handles for the drawers.*

BEFORE

*Helping the dresser shed its multiple layers of paint was brilliant. This stripping operation allowed it to retain its charming antique appearance.*

## INSTALLING THE SINK

**T**wo openings have been made on the top of the dresser to allow for the insertion of the sink and faucets. The sink simply has to be dropped into place. For this type of job, it is recommended that the plumbing come through the wall and not through the floor, otherwise it might be visible. You also need to drill holes at the back of the dresser for the pipes to fit through.